PRINCEWILL LAGANG

The Christian Dating Playbook: Strategies for Success

First published by PRINCEWILL LAGANG 2023

Copyright © 2023 by Princewill Lagang

All rights reserved. No part of this publication may be reproduced, stored or transmitted in any form or by any means, electronic, mechanical, photocopying, recording, scanning, or otherwise without written permission from the publisher. It is illegal to copy this book, post it to a website, or distribute it by any other means without permission.

Princewill Lagang asserts the moral right to be identified as the author of this work.

First edition

This book was professionally typeset on Reedsy. Find out more at reedsy.com

Contents

1	Understanding Your Game	1
2	Building a Solid Foundation	5
3	Seeking Connection	9
4	Navigating Challenges and Red Flags	13
5	Fostering Intimacy and Growth	17
6	Preparing for a Christ-Centered Future	21
7	Perseverance and Faith in Every Season	25
8	Cultivating a Lasting Love	29
9	Enriching Your Christian Love Story	33
10	Writing Your Everlasting Love Story	37
11	Passing the Torch of Faith	41
12	The Journey Continues	45

1

Understanding Your Game

Title: "The Christian Dating Playbook: Strategies for Success"

Introduction

In a world filled with ever-evolving norms, expectations, and digital connections, finding love as a Christian can be both a challenging and rewarding journey. "The Christian Dating Playbook: Strategies for Success" is your comprehensive guide to navigating the complex world of dating while staying true to your faith. This book will provide you with a step-by-step approach to Christian dating, helping you build meaningful connections, navigate potential pitfalls, and ultimately find a partner who shares your values and beliefs.

Section 1: The Foundation

Chapter 1: Understanding Your Game

"Before you step onto the field, you need to understand the rules of the game." This chapter sets the stage for your journey towards successful Christian dating by helping you understand the key principles that underpin this endeavor.

1.1 The Importance of Faith

In the realm of Christian dating, faith is your North Star. Your relationship with God is not just a part of your life; it's the core of your identity. Understanding the significance of faith will not only guide your choices but also ensure that your partner shares this fundamental value.

1.2 Defining Success

Success in Christian dating is not just about finding a partner, but finding the right partner. In this section, you will explore what success means to you personally, helping you set clear, faith-based dating goals that align with your values and long-term vision.

1.3 Honoring Your Values

Your faith comes with a set of values that guide your behavior. In this section, you will reflect on your values and how they influence your choices in dating. This self-awareness will be the cornerstone of your dating strategy.

Section 2: The Preparation

Chapter 2: Building Your Team

Dating is not a solo endeavor; you'll need a support system to navigate the challenges and celebrate the successes. In this chapter, you will learn how to build your dating support team, including friends, family, mentors, and your spiritual community.

2.1 Friends as Allies

Your friends can provide invaluable insights, encouragement, and accountability. Learn how to choose the right friends to confide in and how to communicate with them about your dating journey.

2.2 Family's Role

Your family plays a significant role in your life, and their input matters. Discover how to involve your family in your dating life while maintaining healthy boundaries.

2.3 Mentors and Spiritual Advisors

Seeking guidance from experienced individuals or spiritual leaders can offer you profound wisdom and perspective. This chapter will guide you on finding the right mentors and advisors for your unique journey.

Section 3: The Game Plan

Chapter 3: Finding Potential Matches

Now that you have established your foundation and built your support team, it's time to start searching for potential matches who share your Christian faith and values.

3.1 The Online Dating World

With the rise of technology, online dating is a popular option for many. Explore the world of online dating, including creating an authentic online profile and navigating potential pitfalls.

3.2 Offline Opportunities

In-person connections remain crucial in the dating process. Discover how to create opportunities to meet like-minded individuals within your community, church, or through social activities.

3.3 What to Look For

Learn how to identify potential partners who align with your values and long-term vision. This chapter will provide you with a checklist of qualities and attributes to consider.

Conclusion

In Chapter 1, you've laid the groundwork for a successful Christian dating journey. You've understood the importance of faith, defined your version of success, and embraced your core values. You've also started building your support system and learned how to find potential matches.

"The Christian Dating Playbook" is your playbook for success, and the chapters that follow will equip you with practical strategies, tips, and insights to make your dating journey an enriching and fulfilling experience. With faith as your guide, you are well on your way to finding a love that not only complements your life but also enriches your spiritual journey.

2

Building a Solid Foundation

Title: "The Christian Dating Playbook: Strategies for Success"

Introduction

Chapter 2, "Building a Solid Foundation," delves deeper into the core principles of successful Christian dating. In this chapter, we will explore the essential elements that form the bedrock of a lasting, faith-centered relationship. A strong foundation is crucial, as it not only supports the growth of your relationship but also helps it withstand the inevitable challenges that may come your way.

Section 1: Self-Discovery

Chapter 2.1: Knowing Thyself

To build a solid foundation for your Christian dating journey, you must first understand and accept yourself. This chapter focuses on the importance of self-discovery and provides you with practical tools to explore your identity, values, and personal goals.

2.1.1 Self-Reflection

Embark on a journey of self-reflection, understanding your strengths, weaknesses, and your unique qualities that make you an attractive partner.

2.1.2 Clarifying Your Faith

Dive deeper into your faith, and understand how your beliefs influence your daily life, choices, and expectations in a partner.

2.1.3 Personal Goals

Define your short-term and long-term life goals and aspirations, both within and outside the context of a relationship. Your personal goals should align with your faith and values.

Section 2: Emotional Health

Chapter 2.2: Emotional Intelligence

Emotional intelligence is a vital component of any healthy relationship. This chapter delves into the world of emotions, teaching you how to navigate them and how to establish open and honest communication with potential partners.

2.2.1 Understanding Emotions

Learn to identify and understand your own emotions, as well as the emotions of others. Emotional awareness is key to fostering a healthy connection.

2.2.2 Effective Communication

Effective communication is essential in a Christian relationship. Discover how to express your feelings, thoughts, and expectations with kindness, empathy, and honesty.

2.2.3 Handling Rejection and Disappointment

Rejection and disappointment are part of the dating journey. This chapter provides guidance on how to cope with these challenges in a healthy and faith-centered manner.

Section 3: Relationship Goals

Chapter 2.3: Defining Relationship Goals

This chapter focuses on setting clear, faith-based relationship goals and understanding what you desire in a partner. Your relationship goals will serve as a compass for your Christian dating journey.

2.3.1 Core Relationship Values

Identify the values and principles that are non-negotiable for you in a Christian relationship. These will help you make informed choices and establish boundaries.

2.3.2 Long-Term Vision

Consider your long-term vision for a Christian partnership, encompassing aspects such as marriage, family, and spiritual growth. These dreams will guide your choices and actions.

2.3.3 Compatibility Assessment

Evaluate potential partners based on your core values and long-term vision, ensuring that there is alignment and compatibility.

Conclusion

In this chapter, you've laid the foundation for your Christian dating journey. You've embarked on a journey of self-discovery, honed your emotional intelligence, and defined your relationship goals. Armed with this self-awareness and a clear understanding of what you're looking for in a partner, you're now prepared to move forward into the exciting world of Christian dating.

With a solid foundation in place, you're better equipped to make wise choices, communicate effectively, and build a relationship that is not only grounded in faith but also fulfilling and lasting. The strategies outlined in this chapter will help you navigate the complexities of Christian dating with confidence and purpose.

3

Seeking Connection

Title: "The Christian Dating Playbook: Strategies for Success"

Introduction

As you progress through "The Christian Dating Playbook," you've established a solid foundation and built self-awareness, emotional intelligence, and relationship goals. Now, in Chapter 3, "Seeking Connection," you'll explore the practical steps to initiate meaningful connections and navigate the world of Christian dating with purpose and intention.

Section 1: Making the First Move

Chapter 3.1: Initiating Contact

The first step in any dating journey is initiating contact. This chapter provides guidance on how to make the first move and reach out to potential matches, whether online or in person.

3.1.1 Online Initiatives

Learn how to craft thoughtful, faith-centered messages when using online dating platforms, making a positive first impression.

3.1.2 In-Person Approaches

Discover strategies for approaching someone you're interested in at events, gatherings, or your faith community, always respecting boundaries and consent.

3.1.3 Communication Etiquette

Understand the importance of clear and respectful communication, ensuring your interactions reflect your Christian values.

Section 2: Building Connection

Chapter 3.2: Cultivating Conversations

Once you've made the initial contact, this chapter guides you in cultivating meaningful conversations that foster a deeper connection and understanding.

3.2.1 Active Listening

Develop the art of active listening, which will help you understand your potential partner's values, beliefs, and emotions.

3.2.2 Open-Ended Questions

Learn to ask open-ended questions that encourage thoughtful responses and create opportunities for more profound conversations.

3.2.3 Sharing Your Faith

Find ways to incorporate discussions about your faith into your conversations, so you can gauge your potential partner's spiritual compatibility.

Section 3: Navigating Challenges

Chapter 3.3: Addressing Differences

Every relationship faces challenges, and in the Christian dating journey, addressing differences in beliefs, values, and expectations is crucial. This chapter equips you to handle these challenges with grace and understanding.

3.3.1 Conflict Resolution

Learn effective conflict resolution strategies that align with your Christian values, ensuring disagreements are opportunities for growth, not division.

3.3.2 Balancing Individuality and Togetherness

Explore how to strike a balance between maintaining your individual identity and building a strong connection with your partner.

3.3.3 Maintaining Boundaries

Understand the significance of setting and respecting boundaries in a Christian relationship, helping to safeguard your emotional and spiritual well-being.

Conclusion

Chapter 3, "Seeking Connection," takes you further into the Christian dating journey, from making the first move to cultivating conversations and addressing challenges. With the tools and strategies outlined in this chapter, you'll be well-equipped to approach potential matches with authenticity, engage in meaningful dialogues, and handle differences with grace and faith-centered wisdom.

As you progress through the playbook, remember that building a meaningful Christian relationship is a process that requires time, patience, and dedication. The strategies and insights provided in this chapter will help you lay the groundwork for a strong and faith-centered connection, setting the stage for the deeper exploration of Christian dating in the chapters to come.

4

Navigating Challenges and Red Flags

Title: "The Christian Dating Playbook: Strategies for Success"

Introduction

In Chapter 4, "Navigating Challenges and Red Flags," we address the realities of Christian dating. As you journey toward a faith-centered relationship, it's essential to recognize and respond to challenges and potential warning signs. This chapter equips you with the wisdom and discernment needed to maintain a healthy, Christ-centered connection.

Section 1: Identifying Challenges

Chapter 4.1: Common Dating Challenges

In this section, we explore challenges that frequently arise during the dating process and provide strategies for addressing them within the context of your faith.

4.1.1 Communication Breakdowns

Learn how to navigate miscommunications, misunderstandings, and other communication challenges that can arise in Christian relationships.

4.1.2 Family and Cultural Differences

Discover how to handle differences in family background, cultural traditions, and expectations, while remaining true to your faith.

4.1.3 Balancing Time and Priorities

Explore strategies for maintaining a healthy balance between your relationship, personal goals, and faith commitments.

Section 2: Recognizing Red Flags

Chapter 4.2: Warning Signs

Understanding and responding to red flags is vital to protect your emotional, spiritual, and relational well-being. This chapter helps you identify and address warning signs.

4.2.1 Misaligned Values

Learn to recognize when your potential partner's values and beliefs significantly differ from yours, which could lead to future conflicts.

4.2.2 Lack of Respect

Discover how to identify signs of disrespect, such as dismissive attitudes or boundary violations, and address them appropriately.

4.2.3 Trust and Honesty Issues

NAVIGATING CHALLENGES AND RED FLAGS

Recognize the importance of trust and honesty in a Christian relationship, and know how to address issues of secrecy or dishonesty.

Section 3: Strategies for Navigating Challenges

Chapter 4.3: Resolving Conflicts

In any relationship, conflicts are inevitable. This section offers guidance on resolving disagreements in a way that upholds Christian values and strengthens your connection.

4.3.1 Seeking Guidance

Learn when and how to seek guidance from mentors, pastors, or trusted individuals within your faith community when facing significant relationship challenges.

4.3.2 Faith-Centered Conflict Resolution

Explore strategies for resolving conflicts in a way that aligns with your faith, emphasizing forgiveness, reconciliation, and understanding.

4.3.3 Setting Boundaries

Understand the importance of maintaining boundaries to protect your emotional and spiritual well-being, and learn to communicate these boundaries effectively.

Conclusion

Chapter 4, "Navigating Challenges and Red Flags," equips you with the tools and knowledge needed to address common relationship challenges and recognize red flags that may threaten the health and stability of your faith-centered relationship. By understanding these challenges and having a plan for addressing them, you can navigate the dating journey with greater confidence and discernment.

Remember that challenges and red flags are a part of any relationship, and how you respond to them will shape the course of your connection. The strategies in this chapter are designed to help you maintain a strong, faith-centered bond while addressing any issues that may arise along the way.

5

Fostering Intimacy and Growth

Title: "The Christian Dating Playbook: Strategies for Success"

Introduction

In Chapter 5, "Fostering Intimacy and Growth," we explore the deeper aspects of Christian dating, focusing on the development of intimacy and personal growth within your relationship. This chapter delves into the spiritual and emotional bonds that form the foundation of a lasting, faith-centered connection.

Section 1: Building Spiritual Intimacy

Chapter 5.1: Nurturing Your Faith Together

This section delves into the ways you and your partner can cultivate a strong, shared spiritual life, deepening your connection through faith.

5.1.1 Worshiping Together

Learn the significance of attending church and engaging in spiritual practices as a couple, and discover how it can strengthen your bond.

5.1.2 Prayer and Reflection

Explore how prayer, meditation, and spiritual reflection can become a source of intimacy and growth in your relationship.

5.1.3 Studying Scripture

Discover the benefits of studying the Bible together, and how it can provide insights and guidance for your relationship.

Section 2: Emotional Intimacy

Chapter 5.2: Developing Emotional Connection

Emotional intimacy is a vital aspect of a healthy relationship. This section offers strategies to deepen your emotional connection.

5.2.1 Vulnerability and Trust

Learn the art of vulnerability, how to build trust, and why sharing your fears, dreams, and insecurities is essential for emotional intimacy.

5.2.2 Active Listening and Empathy

Understand the power of active listening and empathy in nurturing emotional connection, as well as how to strengthen these skills.

5.2.3 Conflict Resolution with Grace

Building emotional intimacy also involves resolving conflicts gracefully, ensuring that challenges lead to growth rather than division.

Section 3: Personal and Relationship Growth

Chapter 5.3: Growing Together

This section focuses on the individual and collective growth that takes place within a Christian relationship.

5.3.1 Setting Mutual Goals

Learn to set goals as a couple, which will guide your shared vision for the future and help you grow together.

5.3.2 Balancing Independence and Togetherness

Discover strategies for balancing your individuality and independence with your commitment to building a shared life.

5.3.3 Embracing Change

Understand how personal and relational growth involves embracing change, adapting to life's challenges, and staying connected through the ups and downs.

Conclusion

Chapter 5, "Fostering Intimacy and Growth," focuses on the spiritual and emotional aspects of your faith-centered relationship. By building spiritual intimacy, nurturing emotional connection, and promoting personal and relational growth, you'll not only deepen your bond but also continue to align your relationship with your Christian values.

As you progress through "The Christian Dating Playbook," remember that fostering intimacy and growth is a lifelong journey. By investing in the spiritual and emotional aspects of your relationship, you're building a strong, faith-centered foundation for the future and creating a love that is not only enduring but also enriching.

6

Preparing for a Christ-Centered Future

Title: "The Christian Dating Playbook: Strategies for Success"

Introduction

In Chapter 6, "Preparing for a Christ-Centered Future," we take a closer look at the steps necessary to transition from dating to a more committed, Christ-centered relationship. This chapter is dedicated to helping you prepare for the future, where your faith continues to be the guiding light of your journey together.

Section 1: Discerning Commitment

Chapter 6.1: Moving Towards Commitment

As your relationship evolves, you'll need to discern whether it's time to move toward a more committed phase. This section helps you navigate this significant decision.

6.1.1 Signs of Readiness

Explore the signs that indicate you and your partner are ready for a more committed relationship, such as shared values, emotional connection, and common goals.

6.1.2 Communicating Intent

Learn how to have open and honest conversations about your intentions and expectations, ensuring both partners are on the same page.

6.1.3 Seeking Spiritual Guidance

Consider the role of seeking spiritual guidance, such as pre-marital counseling or pastoral advice, to assist in making this transition.

Section 2: Preparing for Marriage

Chapter 6.2: The Path to Marriage

This section focuses on the journey toward marriage, providing practical steps and advice for preparing for a Christ-centered marriage.

6.2.1 Premarital Counseling

Understand the importance of premarital counseling in addressing potential issues, setting expectations, and ensuring a strong foundation for your marriage.

6.2.2 Planning a Christ-Centered Ceremony

Explore the elements of a Christ-centered wedding ceremony and the importance of incorporating your faith into the celebration.

6.2.3 Financial Planning and Stewardship

Discuss the financial aspects of marriage, including budgeting, financial transparency, and stewardship of resources.

Section 3: Nurturing a Faith-Centered Marriage

Chapter 6.3: Sustaining Your Christ-Centered Marriage

This section provides insights into how to sustain a faith-centered marriage once you've taken that step, with a focus on maintaining the spiritual and emotional aspects of your relationship.

6.3.1 Daily Devotionals

Discover the benefits of daily devotionals and how they can keep your faith at the forefront of your marriage.

6.3.2 Community and Support

Understand the importance of maintaining your connection to your faith community and seeking support when needed.

6.3.3 Relationship Enrichment

Explore strategies for continually enriching your relationship through shared experiences, communication, and love.

Conclusion

Chapter 6, "Preparing for a Christ-Centered Future," addresses the transition from dating to a more committed, faith-centered relationship, with a focus on marriage. By discerning commitment, preparing for marriage, and nurturing a faith-centered marriage, you are taking steps to ensure that your love remains deeply rooted in your Christian values and continues to grow in strength and depth.

As you move forward on this journey, remember that your faith will remain a guiding force in your relationship, and the strategies presented in this chapter are designed to help you build a strong foundation for a Christ-centered future together.

7

Perseverance and Faith in Every Season

Title: "The Christian Dating Playbook: Strategies for Success"

Introduction

In Chapter 7, "Perseverance and Faith in Every Season," we explore the importance of resilience, faith, and commitment as you navigate the various seasons and challenges that come with a faith-centered relationship. This chapter will equip you with strategies to maintain a Christ-centered connection throughout life's changes.

Section 1: Seasons of Change

Chapter 7.1: Navigating Life's Transitions

Life is marked by seasons of change, and your relationship will experience them too. This section provides guidance on how to navigate and grow through these shifts while remaining faithful to your Christian values.

7.1.1 Marriage and Family

Explore the challenges and joys that come with marriage and starting a family, including the importance of keeping faith at the center of these significant life changes.

7.1.2 Career and Personal Growth

Learn to support each other's personal and professional growth, acknowledging the role faith plays in your individual aspirations.

7.1.3 Loss and Grief

Addressing the difficulties of loss and grief with faith, including how to lean on your spiritual community for support.

Section 2: Perseverance and Resilience

Chapter 7.2: Building Resilience

Resilience is vital in maintaining a faith-centered relationship through life's ups and downs. This section focuses on strategies for building emotional and spiritual resilience together.

7.2.1 Prayer and Faith Practices

Discover how maintaining a strong connection with your faith through prayer, scripture, and spiritual practices can sustain you during challenging times.

7.2.2 Communication in Times of Crisis

Explore the importance of open and honest communication when facing difficulties, and how it can strengthen your bond.

7.2.3 Seeking Professional Help

Understand when and how to seek professional guidance, such as counseling or therapy, to address relationship challenges and maintain your Christian values.

Section 3: Celebrating Milestones

Chapter 7.3: Recognizing and Celebrating Achievements

Even amid challenges, it's essential to acknowledge and celebrate your achievements and milestones together. This section offers strategies for appreciating your journey and deepening your faith-centered bond.

7.3.1 Expressing Gratitude

Learn the art of expressing gratitude and thankfulness to God for your relationship and the journey you've shared.

7.3.2 Honoring Anniversaries and Milestones

Explore ways to celebrate your relationship's milestones, such as anniversaries, with a focus on faith and love.

7.3.3 Sharing Your Journey

Consider how sharing your relationship story with others can inspire and encourage those around you while reaffirming your faith.

Conclusion

Chapter 7, "Perseverance and Faith in Every Season," reminds you that a faith-centered relationship is an enduring commitment that requires perseverance, faith, and resilience in the face of life's changes and challenges. By navigating seasons of change, building emotional and spiritual resilience, and celebrating achievements, you can strengthen your bond and continue to align your relationship with your Christian values.

As you journey forward, remember that your faith is the constant thread that runs through your relationship, guiding you through every season and helping you build a love that remains steadfast and true.

8

Cultivating a Lasting Love

Title: "The Christian Dating Playbook: Strategies for Success"

Introduction

In Chapter 8, "Cultivating a Lasting Love," we explore the keys to nurturing and sustaining a love that endures the test of time within the context of Christian dating. This chapter will provide you with insights and practical strategies to help you cultivate a deep, lasting, and faith-centered relationship.

Section 1: The Art of Connection

Chapter 8.1: Continuously Connecting

Sustaining a lasting love requires an ongoing commitment to connection. This section focuses on various ways to continue building a strong and intimate bond.

8.1.1 Quality Time

Discover the significance of spending quality time together, whether through date nights, shared hobbies, or quiet moments of reflection.

8.1.2 Emotional Presence

Learn how to be emotionally present for your partner, offering support, understanding, and empathy during both joyous and challenging times.

8.1.3 Expressing Affection

Explore the importance of physical and verbal affection in maintaining a loving connection.

Section 2: Growing Spiritually Together

Chapter 8.2: Nurturing Spiritual Growth

Spiritual growth is a cornerstone of a lasting Christian relationship. This section provides guidance on how to nurture spiritual growth together.

8.2.1 Prayer and Worship

Discover the beauty of praying together, attending worship services, and deepening your spiritual connection as a couple.

8.2.2 Faith-Based Study and Reflection

Engage in faith-based study, reflection, and discussion that enriches your spiritual journey as individuals and as a couple.

8.2.3 Serving Others

Explore opportunities to serve together, whether through volunteering, missions, or other acts of Christian service that strengthen your bond and faith.

Section 3: Overcoming Challenges

Chapter 8.3: Resilience in the Face of Challenges

Every relationship faces difficulties, but it's how you navigate them that truly matters. This section focuses on strategies for resilience in the face of challenges.

8.3.1 Forgiveness and Reconciliation

Understand the importance of forgiveness and reconciliation, drawing from your Christian faith to heal rifts and move forward.

8.3.2 Seeking Guidance and Support

Learn how to lean on your faith community, mentors, and professional help when facing relationship challenges, ensuring you maintain a faith-centered approach to resolution.

8.3.3 Staying True to Your Values

Explore ways to remain true to your Christian values even when faced with difficult decisions or external pressures.

Conclusion

Chapter 8, "Cultivating a Lasting Love," brings you to the culmination of your Christian dating journey. By consistently connecting, nurturing spiritual growth, and demonstrating resilience in the face of challenges, you can cultivate a love that endures the test of time and aligns with your Christian values.

As you continue to walk this path, remember that your relationship is a journey, and maintaining a lasting love requires a daily commitment to growth, connection, and faith. With the strategies and insights provided in this chapter, you are well-equipped to cultivate a deep, faith-centered love that will stand the test of time.

9

Enriching Your Christian Love Story

Title: "The Christian Dating Playbook: Strategies for Success"

Introduction

In Chapter 9, "Enriching Your Christian Love Story," we explore how to elevate your faith-centered relationship to new heights. This chapter is dedicated to adding depth, joy, and spiritual richness to your love story. By integrating these strategies, you can create a love that truly reflects your Christian values.

Section 1: Fostering Joy and Adventure

Chapter 9.1: Embracing Joy in Everyday Life

Happiness and joy are essential elements of a lasting relationship. In this section, we'll discuss ways to infuse your relationship with joy and adventure.

9.1.1 Celebrating the Little Things

Learn the art of celebrating the small moments in your relationship, fostering gratitude and happiness.

9.1.2 Exploring New Experiences

Discover the benefits of trying new activities, going on adventures, and expanding your horizons together.

9.1.3 Laughter and Playfulness

Explore the role of laughter, humor, and playfulness in strengthening your bond and bringing joy into your relationship.

Section 2: Sustaining Passion and Romance

Chapter 9.2: Keeping the Flame Alive

Passion and romance are vital components of a thriving love story. This section provides strategies for keeping the flame of love alive and burning brightly.

9.2.1 Date Nights and Intimacy

Explore the significance of regular date nights, intimacy, and maintaining the romantic spark in your relationship.

9.2.2 Acts of Love and Affection

Discover ways to show your love through gestures, surprises, and acts of affection that keep the romance alive.

9.2.3 Communication of Desires

Openly communicate your desires and fantasies to enhance intimacy and deepen the connection with your partner.

Section 3: Enriching Your Spiritual Connection

Chapter 9.3: Deepening Your Faith Together

A faith-centered relationship thrives on a deep spiritual connection. In this section, we'll discuss how to enrich your faith journey as a couple.

9.3.1 Shared Spiritual Practices

Explore the benefits of establishing shared spiritual practices and routines that strengthen your bond.

9.3.2 Retreats and Pilgrimages

Consider the significance of going on retreats or pilgrimages together to deepen your spiritual connection and create lasting memories.

9.3.3 Serving Together

Discover the power of serving together in your faith community or through missions and volunteer work, which can deepen your connection and shared sense of purpose.

Conclusion

Chapter 9, "Enriching Your Christian Love Story," brings you to a stage where you can elevate your faith-centered relationship to new heights. By fostering joy and adventure, sustaining passion and romance, and enriching your spiritual connection, you can create a love story that not only reflects your Christian values but also fills your life with deep joy, lasting passion, and spiritual richness.

As you continue to write your love story, remember that it's a lifelong journey. The strategies and insights provided in this chapter are designed to help you infuse your relationship with love, joy, and faith, creating a love story that becomes a testament to the beauty of faith-centered love.

10

Writing Your Everlasting Love Story

Title: "The Christian Dating Playbook: Strategies for Success"

Introduction

Chapter 10, "Writing Your Everlasting Love Story," marks the culmination of your Christian dating journey. This chapter guides you on how to reflect on the path you've traveled and how to shape the narrative of your relationship's future. By embracing the strategies and insights in this chapter, you'll be empowered to write a love story that reflects your faith, values, and lasting commitment.

Section 1: Reflecting on the Journey

Chapter 10.1: The Pages of Your Past

Before you move forward, it's crucial to look back and reflect on the journey you've undertaken as a couple. This section helps you revisit the important milestones and challenges you've faced.

10.1.1 Celebrating Achievements

Acknowledge your relationship's achievements and the growth you've experienced together, celebrating your shared successes.

10.1.2 Learning from Challenges

Reflect on the challenges you've encountered and the valuable lessons you've gained from them, which have strengthened your bond and faith.

10.1.3 Gratitude and Thankfulness

Express gratitude and thankfulness for the love and support you've found in each other, as well as for the guidance and blessings of your faith.

Section 2: Mapping Your Future

Chapter 10.2: Setting the Course Ahead

This section focuses on the future and how to set goals, aspirations, and intentions that reflect your shared vision for a lasting love story.

10.2.1 Defining Your Future Together

Clarify your vision for your shared future, considering aspects like family, career, and continued spiritual growth.

10.2.2 Goal Setting

Set clear, faith-centered goals as a couple, whether related to your relationship, family, career, or community involvement.

10.2.3 Strengthening Commitment

Reaffirm your commitment to each other and your shared Christian values, recognizing that your faith remains the cornerstone of your love story.

Section 3: Embracing Each Chapter

Chapter 10.3: Living Each Moment

In this section, you'll learn how to embrace each moment of your love story, allowing the narrative to evolve with faith, love, and meaning.

10.3.1 Treasuring Everyday Moments

Discover the beauty of treasuring everyday moments and cultivating a mindful appreciation for the blessings of your relationship.

10.3.2 Overcoming Future Challenges

Prepare for the challenges that may arise in your future, knowing that your faith, love, and commitment will guide you through.

10.3.3 Renewing Love

Understand the importance of renewing your love daily, reinforcing your commitment to each other and your Christian values.

Conclusion

Chapter 10, "Writing Your Everlasting Love Story," is a reflection on your past, a roadmap for your future, and a call to embrace each chapter of your love story with faith and love. By looking back on your journey, setting the course for your shared future, and living each moment with purpose and intention, you have the opportunity to write a love story that stands as a testament to the enduring beauty of Christian love.

Your love story is a work in progress, continually evolving with each passing day. As you write your story, remember that the Christian dating playbook provides you with the strategies and insights needed to create a love story that reflects your faith, values, and lasting commitment, a love story that endures for a lifetime.

11

Passing the Torch of Faith

Title: "The Christian Dating Playbook: Strategies for Success"

Introduction

Chapter 11, "Passing the Torch of Faith," takes you on a journey beyond your own love story. This chapter explores the significance of sharing your faith and relationship wisdom with others, as well as nurturing the spiritual growth of the next generation. By doing so, you'll not only strengthen your own love but also contribute to the legacy of faith-centered relationships.

Section 1: Sharing Your Wisdom

Chapter 11.1: Passing on Relationship Insights

Reflecting on your own relationship journey, this section provides guidance on sharing your relationship insights and wisdom with others.

11.1.1 Mentorship and Counseling

Consider taking on mentorship roles, providing guidance to individuals or couples who seek your relationship wisdom.

11.1.2 Sharing Your Story

Explore the power of sharing your love story and the lessons you've learned, offering hope and inspiration to those on their own journey.

11.1.3 Workshops and Seminars

Consider hosting workshops or seminars where you can impart valuable relationship insights and strategies.

Section 2: Nurturing the Next Generation

Chapter 11.2: Fostering Spiritual Growth

This section focuses on nurturing the spiritual growth of the next generation, whether within your family, faith community, or through volunteer work.

11.2.1 Family Devotionals

Learn the importance of family devotionals and how they can instill faith and values in your children or the younger generation.

11.2.2 Youth and Young Adult Ministry

Consider your involvement in youth and young adult ministry, where you can serve as a role model and guide in matters of faith and relationships.

11.2.3 Volunteer Work and Outreach

Explore opportunities for volunteer work or outreach programs that allow you to pass on your faith and relationship wisdom to those in need.

Section 3: Embracing the Legacy of Faith-Centered Love

Chapter 11.3: Creating a Legacy of Love

This section delves into the legacy you can create by passing on the torch of faith-centered love and relationship wisdom.

11.3.1 Writing and Publications

Consider writing about your relationship journey and insights, whether in books, articles, or blog posts, to reach a broader audience.

11.3.2 Leaving a Faith-Centered Legacy

Explore how to leave a legacy of faith-centered love that continues to impact the lives of others, creating a lasting testimony to the beauty of Christian relationships.

11.3.3 Continuing Your Own Love Story

Recognize that, as you pass on the torch of faith, your own love story continues to evolve, enriched by the act of sharing and giving back.

Conclusion

Chapter 11, "Passing the Torch of Faith," brings your Christian dating journey full circle by encouraging you to share your relationship wisdom and nurture the spiritual growth of the next generation. Your love story is not just about you; it's also about the legacy of faith-centered love you can leave behind.

By sharing your insights, offering guidance, and fostering spiritual growth, you're contributing to the legacy of Christian love and relationships. As you do so, your own love story continues to flourish, inspired by the act of passing on the torch of faith and love to others.

12

The Journey Continues

Title: "The Christian Dating Playbook: Strategies for Success"

Introduction

Chapter 12, "The Journey Continues," is the final chapter in "The Christian Dating Playbook." This chapter marks a new beginning while emphasizing that the journey of faith-centered love never truly ends. It's a reminder that, even as you pass on your wisdom and nurture the spiritual growth of the next generation, your own love story continues to evolve, grow, and deepen. In this concluding chapter, we explore the idea that love and faith are evergreen, always capable of renewal and further enrichment.

Section 1: Renewal and Rediscovery

Chapter 12.1: Rediscovering Your Love

The journey continues with a focus on renewal and rediscovery. This section encourages you to rekindle the flames of your faith-centered relationship and explore new horizons in your love story.

12.1.1 Reviving Romance

Discover strategies for rekindling romance, passion, and intimacy in your relationship, even as you navigate the challenges of life together.

12.1.2 Exploring Shared Interests

Find new shared interests and experiences that can bring fresh excitement and depth to your relationship.

12.1.3 Renewed Commitment

Consider the significance of renewing your commitment to each other and your faith, continually strengthening the bond that brought you together in the first place.

Section 2: The Next Chapter

Chapter 12.2: Embracing Future Chapters

In this section, you'll explore the possibilities of the future and how to approach the next chapters in your love story with faith, joy, and anticipation.

12.2.1 Setting New Goals

Set fresh faith-centered goals and aspirations for the future, taking into account your growth as a couple and as individuals.

12.2.2 Nurturing Faith Together

Continue nurturing your faith together, finding new ways to deepen your spiritual connection and grow as individuals of faith.

12.2.3 Supporting Others

As your love story continues, consider how you can continue to support and mentor others on their own journey to faith-centered love.

Conclusion

Chapter 12, "The Journey Continues," marks a new beginning for your faith-centered love story. It underscores the idea that love and faith are ever-evolving, capable of renewal, rediscovery, and continued growth. As you navigate the next chapters of your love story, remember that your faith remains the guiding light, and the strategies and insights provided in "The Christian Dating Playbook" are tools that can be used throughout the journey.

Your love story is a testament to the enduring beauty of Christian love, a story that continues to unfold with each passing day. By embracing the concepts of renewal, rediscovery, and future anticipation, you can create a love that remains evergreen and ever-enriching.

Book Summary: "The Christian Dating Playbook: Strategies for Success"

"The Christian Dating Playbook: Strategies for Success" is a comprehensive guide that equips individuals with the tools and wisdom to navigate the world of dating while staying true to their Christian values. In this playbook, readers embark on a journey that spans 12 chapters, each focusing on a distinct phase of Christian dating.

The book starts by laying a strong foundation in Chapter 1, emphasizing the importance of self-awareness, values, and relationship goals. It encourages readers to reflect on their faith, their identity, and what they are seeking in a Christian relationship.

Chapter 2 delves into the process of finding potential partners. Readers learn strategies for meeting and connecting with like-minded individuals, both online and in-person, always mindful of Christian values and ethics.

Chapter 3, "Seeking Connection," is dedicated to practical steps in initiating and building meaningful connections. It guides readers on how to approach potential partners with authenticity and navigate the early stages of dating.

As the relationship progresses, Chapter 4 explores how to address challenges and identify red flags. It offers insight into maintaining healthy boundaries and addressing differences in beliefs and values.

Chapter 5 focuses on deepening intimacy and fostering emotional and spiritual growth within the relationship. It emphasizes the significance of nurturing the spiritual connection while balancing individual and collective growth.

In Chapter 6, readers are guided on how to transition from dating to a more committed, Christ-centered relationship. It provides advice on discerning commitment, preparing for marriage, and navigating the early stages of marriage.

Chapter 7, titled "Perseverance and Faith in Every Season," delves into maintaining a faith-centered relationship through life's changes and challenges. It offers strategies for building resilience and sustaining a deep connection.

Chapter 8, "Cultivating a Lasting Love," is all about adding depth, joy, and spiritual richness to a faith-centered relationship. It explores the importance of maintaining joy, passion, and romance as the relationship matures.

Chapter 9, titled "Enriching Your Christian Love Story," takes the relationship to new heights. It discusses ways to infuse the relationship with joy and adventure, sustain passion and romance, and enrich the spiritual connection.

In Chapter 10, readers are encouraged to reflect on the journey, set future goals, and commit to living each moment with faith and intention.

Chapter 11 focuses on passing on the torch of faith, sharing relationship wisdom with others, and nurturing the spiritual growth of the next generation. It encourages readers to contribute to the legacy of faith-centered relationships.

The concluding Chapter 12, "The Journey Continues," emphasizes renewal, rediscovery, and approaching future chapters with faith, joy, and anticipation. It underscores the idea that love and faith are evergreen, capable of renewal and continued growth.

"The Christian Dating Playbook" offers a roadmap for individuals seeking to build and sustain faith-centered relationships. It provides insights, strategies, and guidance at every stage of the journey, ultimately emphasizing the enduring beauty of Christian love. Readers are empowered to write their own love stories that reflect their faith, values, and lasting commitment.

www.ingramcontent.com/pod-product-compliance
Lightning Source LLC
LaVergne TN
LVHW010437070526
838199LV00066B/6050